MINECRAFT

IDEAS

WRITTEN BY
Shari Last
and
Julia March

MODELS BY
Alexander Blais
and
Jonas Kramm

CONTENTS

Get ready for a block building adventure!

ENCHANTING TABLE

Give Minecraft items a magical boost by crafting your own LEGO® Minecraft® enchanting table. Complete the build with a fast-spinning spell book.

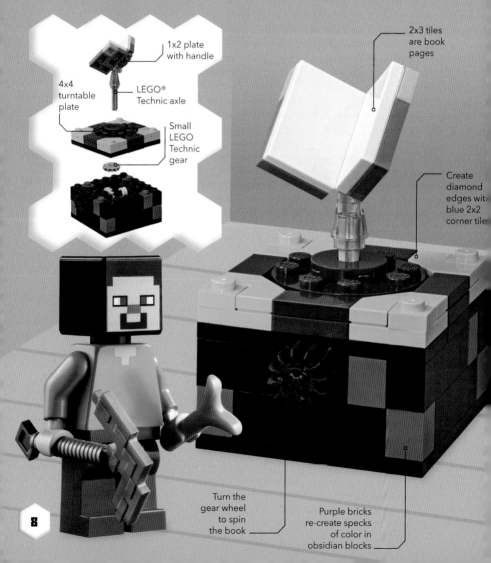

1x2 plate with handle

4x4 turntable plate

LEGO® Technic axle

Small LEGO Technic gear

2x3 tiles are book pages

Create diamond edges with blue 2x2 corner tile

Turn the gear wheel to spin the book

Purple bricks re-create specks of color in obsidian blocks

ROAMING ZOMBIE

Can anyone hear moaning? It's probably this green, grumpy zombie. Build your mob with big, blocky arms and movable legs and let it lumber on.

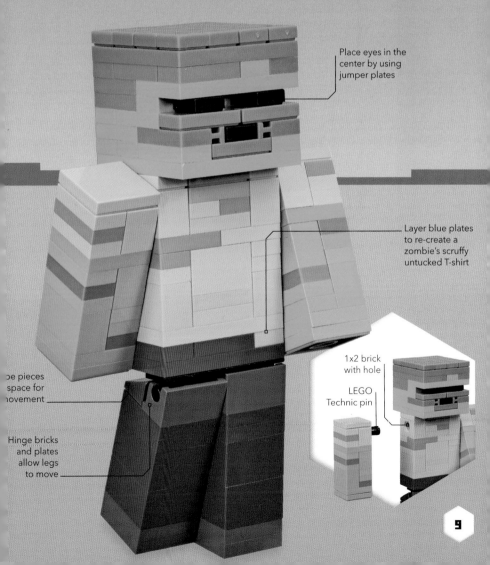

Place eyes in the center by using jumper plates

Layer blue plates to re-create a zombie's scruffy untucked T-shirt

...e pieces
...space for
...ovement

Hinge bricks and plates allow legs to move

1x2 brick with hole

LEGO Technic pin

MINI BIOMES

These micro biomes use small pieces to make a big impression. Build miniature groves, jungles, rivers, and badlands and you'll have the Overworld covered in no time. For extra fun, include some micro characters.

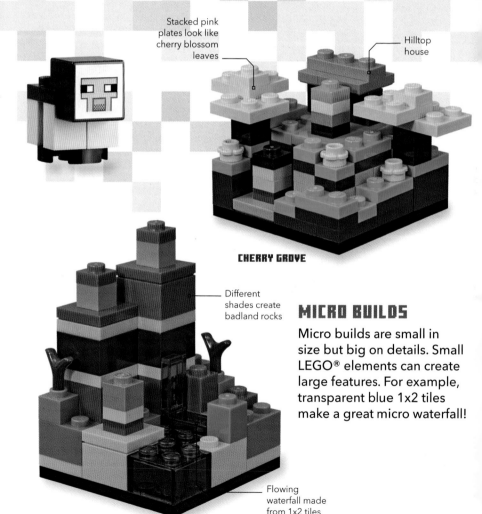

Stacked pink plates look like cherry blossom leaves

Hilltop house

CHERRY GROVE

Different shades create badland rocks

Flowing waterfall made from 1x2 tiles

BADLANDS

MICRO BUILDS

Micro builds are small in size but big on details. Small LEGO® elements can create large features. For example, transparent blue 1x2 tiles make a great micro waterfall!

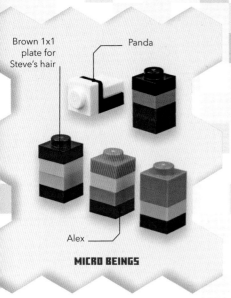

Brown 1x1 plate for Steve's hair

Panda

Alex

MICRO BEINGS

Add white 1x1 tiles to cover trees in snow

Use transparent tiles for ice

FROZEN RIVER

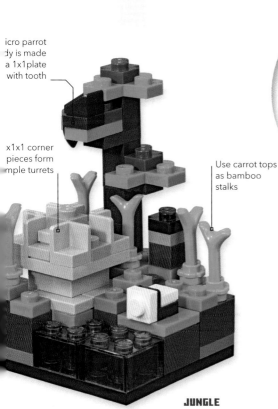

icro parrot dy is made a 1x1 plate with tooth

x1x1 corner pieces form mple turrets

Use carrot tops as bamboo stalks

JUNGLE

TRY THIS

Minecraft worlds are made up of many little environments called biomes. Use tiles and plates to connect multiple mini biomes and create your own micro Minecraft world.

TREASURE MAP

Send your friends hunting for a prize hidden in your Minecraft world with only a LEGO map to guide them. The map uses different colors for the biomes and terrain they must pass through to get to the X.

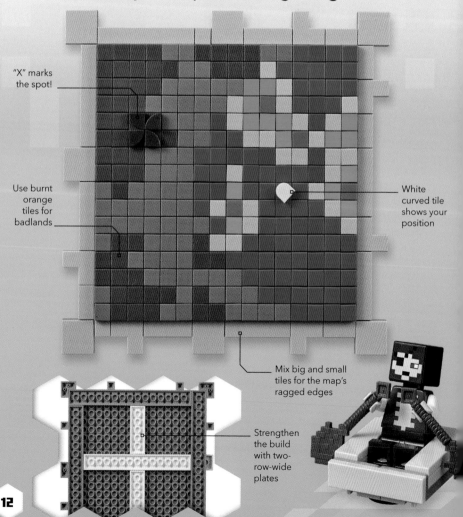

"X" marks the spot!

Use burnt orange tiles for badlands

White curved tile shows your position

Mix big and small tiles for the map's ragged edges

Strengthen the build with two-row-wide plates

FACE YOUR MOBS

Can you baa-lieve how sweet this sheep mob face is? Build more mob faces, either friendly ones, like this sheep and its pals, or hostile ones, like a creeper or Enderman—if you dare.

Raised tiles look like a chicken's blocky beak

Make a sheep's nose by using pink 1x2 tiles

SHEEP

CHICKEN

Create cow markings with different colored tiles

All I need now is a ranch!

Attach tiles and plates to 8x8 plate

COW

HUMONGOUS FUNGUS

This house is as cute as a button—a button mushroom! The mushroom's cap is the roof, and there are two cozy rooms in the stalk. Add a small vegetable patch and you're good to grow.

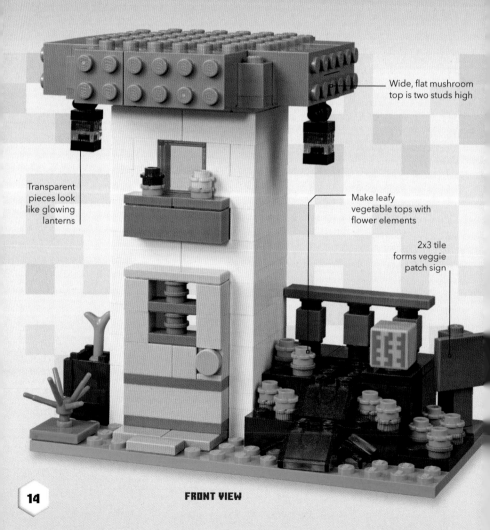

Wide, flat mushroom top is two studs high

Transparent pieces look like glowing lanterns

Make leafy vegetable tops with flower elements

2x3 tile forms veggie patch sign

FRONT VIEW

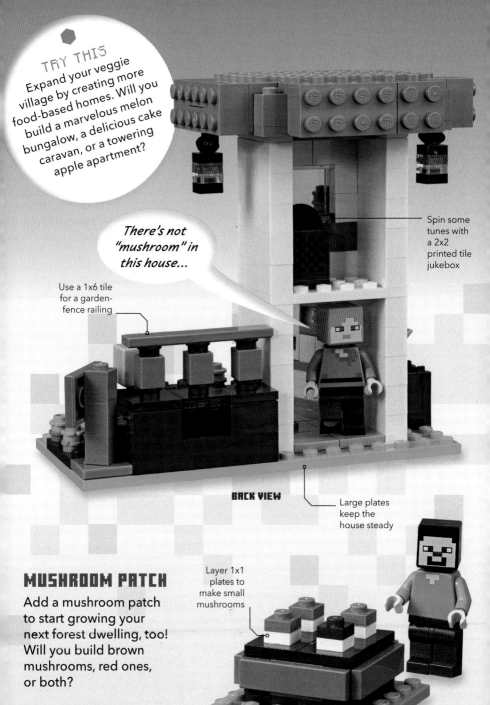

TRY THIS
Expand your veggie village by creating more food-based homes. Will you build a marvelous melon bungalow, a delicious cake caravan, or a towering apple apartment?

Spin some tunes with a 2x2 printed tile jukebox

There's not "mushroom" in this house...

Use a 1x6 tile for a garden-fence railing

BACK VIEW

Large plates keep the house steady

MUSHROOM PATCH

Add a mushroom patch to start growing your next forest dwelling, too! Will you build brown mushrooms, red ones, or both?

Layer 1x1 plates to make small mushrooms

TREE-MENDOUS TREE HOUSE

Your LEGO Minecraft minifigures need a place to relax and hide from exploding creepers. In this big birch treehouse, they can relax and "leaf" their cares behind

Use different shades of green bricks for the leaves

SPECIAL PIECE
This lattice plate is a ladder in this scene, but it can be used as a fence, or even prison window bars. It attaches to the tree trunk with a 1x1 brick with clip.

Attach the lantern using a hose nozzle and plate with clip

Build a cozy beehive with tan 1x2x2 panel walls

That honey looks "bee-licious!"

Bee with clear 1x2 plate wings

MICRO SKY ISLAND

Build this micro island floating in the sky—there's no finer place for a home base. You could look down on your foes, and look out to the amazing views.

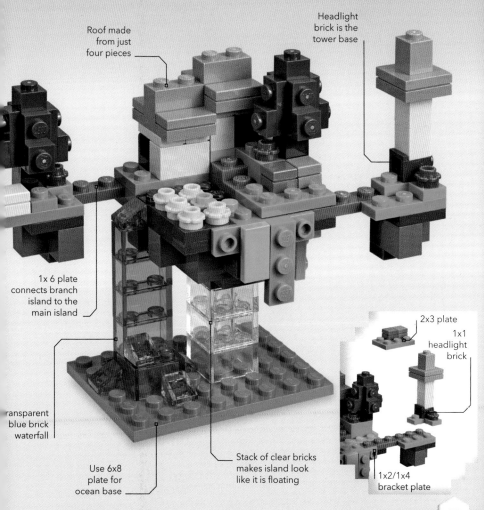

Roof made from just four pieces

Headlight brick is the tower base

1x 6 plate connects branch island to the main island

Transparent blue brick waterfall

Use 6x8 plate for ocean base

Stack of clear bricks makes island look like it is floating

2x3 plate

1x1 headlight brick

1x2/1x4 bracket plate

DOWN IN THE MINE

Would you dare to explore a mineshaft? There could be chests, cobwebs, or even gold underground. Or maybe something—or someone—much scarier...

This mine is mine!

Torches made from LEGO telescope pieces

Who's lurking inside?

Textured bricks frame the mine's opening

Create fences 1x1 bric with bar

CAVE SPIDER

Creepy cave spiders spawn in mineshafts. Use tiles, hinge plates, and bricks to create amazing arachnids.

2x3 tile saddle

CAVE SPIDER

1x2 hinge plates allow legs to move

Chest fits inside minecart

Use darker 1x1 tiles for wheels

MINECART WITH CHEST

TIP

Build a leafy green surface to hide the mine lurking underneath. Use carrot top pieces and brown plates for a grassy biome and white pieces for a snowy one.

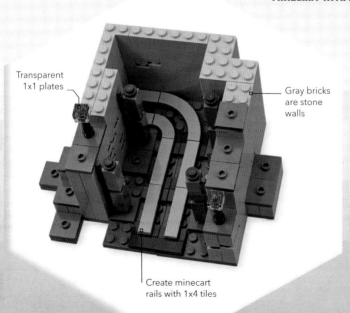

Transparent 1x1 plates

Gray bricks are stone walls

Create minecart rails with 1x4 tiles

FROSTY CABIN

Brrr! It's cold out on the snowy plains. Build this cozy wooden home in the village to keep your minifigures' toes toasty. Why not invite some mobs inside to warm up, too?

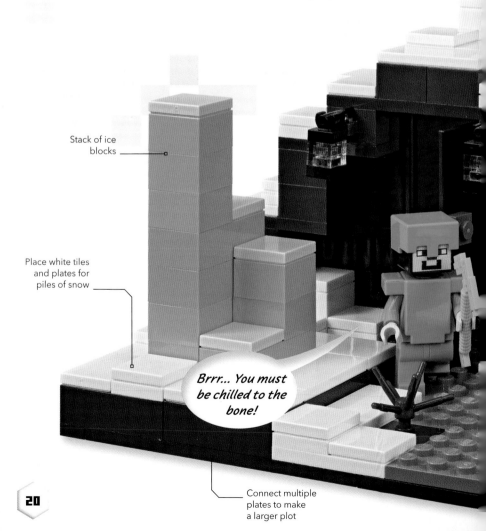

Stack of ice blocks

Place white tiles and plates for piles of snow

Brrr... You must be chilled to the bone!

Connect multiple plates to make a larger plot

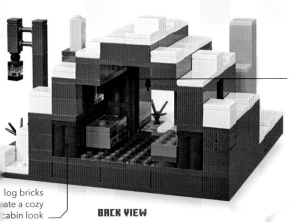

Add a printed
1x2 brick
furnace

log bricks
ate a cozy
cabin look

BACK VIEW

Stacked gray
1x1 bricks make
a chimney

1x1 brick
with side
stud

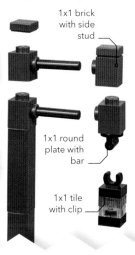

1x1 round
plate with
bar

1x1 tile
with clip

Tall grass peeps
through the snow

Stray with
bow and arrow
at the ready

TIP

Layer plates to show a
variety of terrain. Start with
a brown plate for the earth,
then add green plates for
grass and plants. Top this
with white elements for
freshly fallen snow.

TRY THIS
In Minecraft, pillager outposts consist of several small structures. Use your bricks to build cages, tents, and piles of logs to add to your outpost tower.

Arrange bricks to re-create outpost's arches

Eleg
woo
balust

Fill chest with loot

Decorate the outpost with illager banners

Add green bricks for mossy cobblestone

OUTPOST TOWER

Can your brave minifigures dodge the pillagers in this outpost tower? If so, they can play with the archery equipment, rummage through the treasure, and maybe trap the pillagers in their tower by moving the ladders.

BULLSEYE!

Pillagers and minifigures can practice their archery skills with these dummies. Use yellow bricks with holes for their hay bale bodies.

Printed pumpkin head attaches to jumper plate

Who you calling a dummy?

Arms move on LEGO Technic pin

ARCHERY PRACTICE DUMMIES

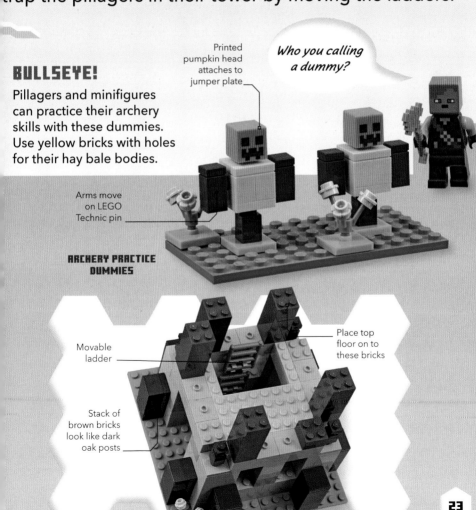

Movable ladder

Place top floor on to these bricks

Stack of brown bricks look like dark oak posts

TRUSTY CHEST

In Minecraft, it isn't wise to leave your items lying around. Store your tools, armor, food, potions, or any other precious objects in this large chest.

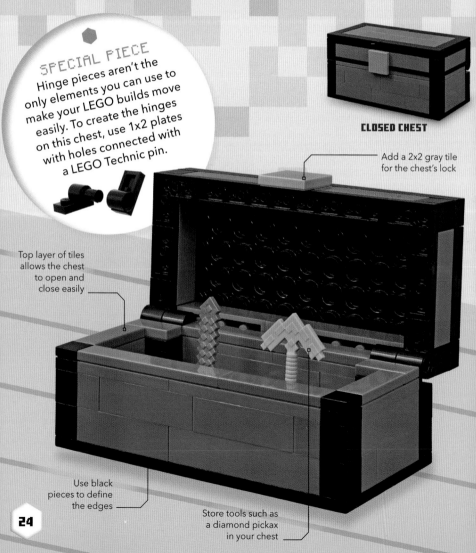

SPECIAL PIECE
Hinge pieces aren't the only elements you can use to make your LEGO builds move easily. To create the hinges on this chest, use 1x2 plates with holes connected with a LEGO Technic pin.

CLOSED CHEST

Add a 2x2 gray tile for the chest's lock

Top layer of tiles allows the chest to open and close easily

Use black pieces to define the edges

Store tools such as a diamond pickax in your chest

24

TNT BAUBLE

Give your festive tree a Minecraft twist with a TNT ornament. For explosive mobs, like a Wither or creeper, it's their favorite winter decoration!

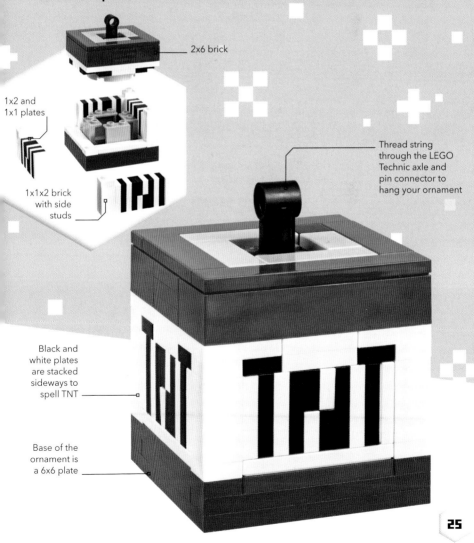

2x6 brick

1x2 and 1x1 plates

1x1x2 brick with side studs

Thread string through the LEGO Technic axle and pin connector to hang your ornament

Black and white plates are stacked sideways to spell TNT

Base of the ornament is a 6x6 plate

FIERCE FRIEND

This long-armed, strong-armed hero is a menace to monsters but a friend to innocent villagers. Don't forget its red poppy, a token of friendship.

Build nose on front of face for a 3D effect

Use black and red 1x1 plates for the eyes

2x3 plate

1x2 bricks

Green and yellow plates are vines

Red poppy is made from a plant base and round plate with petals

Make legs wide and sturdy enough to stand on

LEGO Technic axle allows leg movement

DIAMOND SWORD

The diamond sword is one of the most powerful weapons in Minecraft. Build this LEGO version and be ready for hostile mobs everywhere.

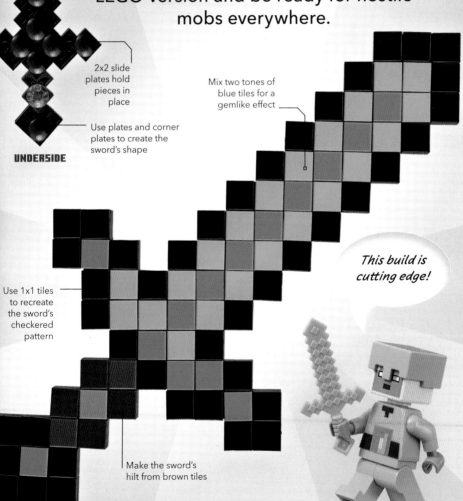

2x2 slide plates hold pieces in place

Mix two tones of blue tiles for a gemlike effect

Use plates and corner plates to create the sword's shape

UNDERSIDE

This build is cutting edge!

Use 1x1 tiles to recreate the sword's checkered pattern

Make the sword's hilt from brown tiles

BUILDING BLOCKS

Minecraft blocks are the basic units that allow you to craft your own unique and fantastic Minecraft world. See if you can recreate your favorite blocks in miniature, using LEGO pieces.

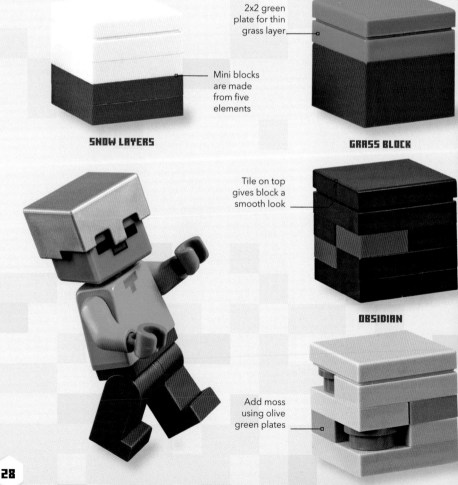

2x2 green plate for thin grass layer

Mini blocks are made from five elements

SNOW LAYERS

GRASS BLOCK

Tile on top gives block a smooth look

OBSIDIAN

Add moss using olive green plates

MOSSY COBBLESTONE

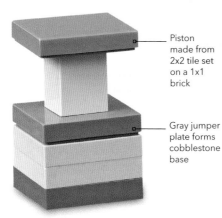

Piston made from 2x2 tile set on a 1x1 brick

Gray jumper plate forms cobblestone base

PISTON

TRY THIS

Use your miniature blocks to create larger builds, just like in Minecraft. Swap the tiles on top of the blocks with plates and then connect the blocks, as you would in the game.

Transparent pieces "glow" like lava

LAVA

1x1 round plates give the ore a crumbled appearance

DIAMOND ORE

Back to square one!

1x2 textured brick looks like wooden planks

BIRCH PLANKS

ROCKY RIDE

This runaway minecart gives passengers a wild ride, hurtling through caves and past obstacles. Scream if you want to go faster (or maybe just to get off).

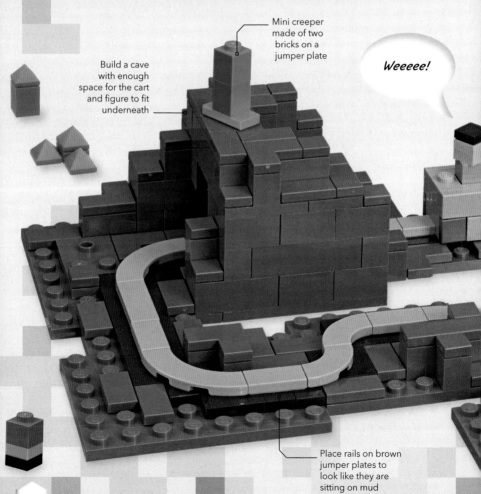

Mini creeper made of two bricks on a jumper plate

Build a cave with enough space for the cart and figure to fit underneath

Weeeee!

Place rails on brown jumper plates to look like they are sitting on mud

Microfigure sits between two 1x1 bricks

OVERHEAD VIEW

Create a curve in the track with a 4x4 round corner tile

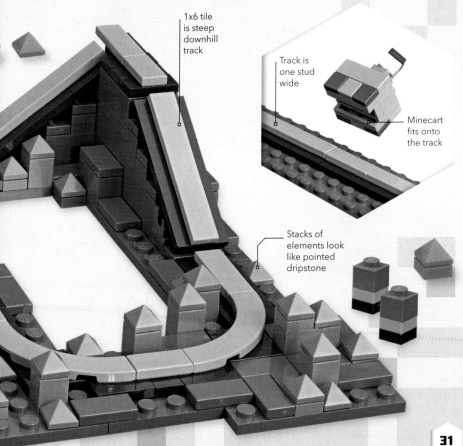

1x6 tile is steep downhill track

Track is one stud wide

Minecart fits onto the track

Stacks of elements look like pointed dripstone

GEODES ROCK!

This mining minifigure is on a mission to find rare objects. Build them a stone geode with glittering amethyst bricks inside to discover. What a lucky break

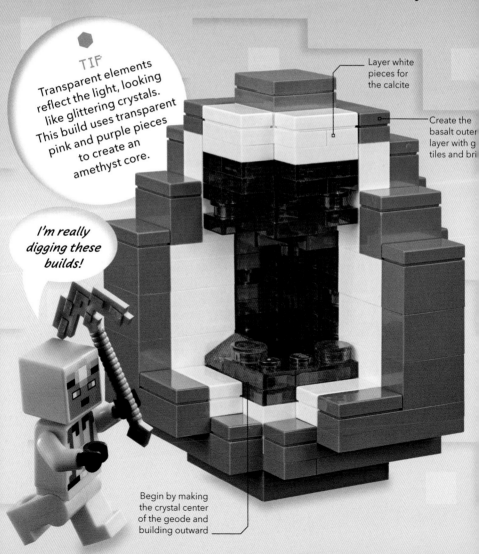

TIP
Transparent elements reflect the light, looking like glittering crystals. This build uses transparent pink and purple pieces to create an amethyst core.

Layer white pieces for the calcite

Create the basalt outer layer with g tiles and bri

I'm really digging these builds!

Begin by making the crystal center of the geode and building outward

TEMPERATE FROG

Jump right into this frog build. This friendly frog is from a temperate swamp, so it has orange skin. It can open its mouth, ready for a cheery croak.

Croak!

Bulging brick eyes

Shape hind legs around the body

Wide, flat feet for stability

Brown tiles d bricks make friendly smile

Plates with clips and bars work as a hinge

1x4 tile

1x1 tile

1x2 plate with ball socket

1x2 plate with ball joint

A DAY AT THE BEACH

For minifigures in need of a break, this beach build is a shore thing. It has sea, sand, a jetty, and even a turtle-spotting zombie. Or maybe that's a zombie-spotting turtle.

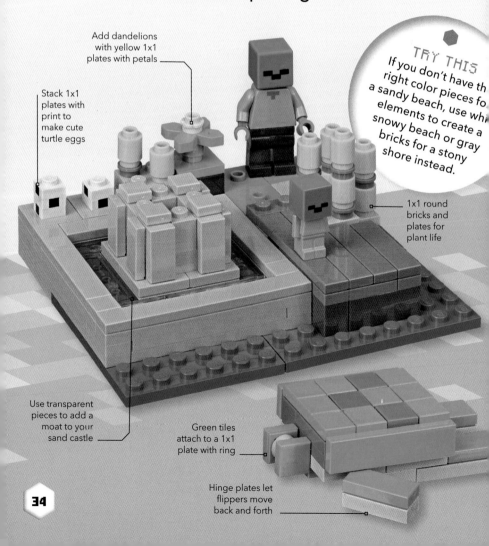

Add dandelions with yellow 1x1 plates with petals

Stack 1x1 plates with print to make cute turtle eggs

TRY THIS
If you don't have the right color pieces for a sandy beach, use white elements to create a snowy beach or gray bricks for a stony shore instead.

1x1 round bricks and plates for plant life

Use transparent pieces to add a moat to your sand castle

Green tiles attach to a 1x1 plate with ring

Hinge plates let flippers move back and forth

PERFECT PUMPKIN

Forget green vegetables—your square, orange LEGO®
Minecraft® pumpkin will be the pick of the patch. It's the
perfect ingredient for fall decorations and games.

1x4 dark orange
plates are
pumpkin ribs

Use 1x1x2
bricks to
build the
corners

6x6 plate
forms the
base and
lid of the
pumpkin

TRY THIS
Transform your great
gourd into a carved pumpkin.
Rebuild one side of the
model using black or brown
pieces to create a grinning
face and orange pieces
to fill in the gaps.

BUILD YOUR OWN ADVENTURE

Craft your own thrilling Minecraft story. Will it be a daring rescue, a hunt for hidden treasure, or a blistering battle between rival mobs? That's up to you

JUNGLE EXPLORER

SKELETON

TRY THIS
Why not take a fairytale and give it a Minecraft twist. Maybe Alex will climb the beanstalk and find a Wither or the jungle explorer will leave her pickax at the ball!

PICKAX

EGG

TNT BLOCK

Minifigure is the hero of the story

PICNIC GARDEN

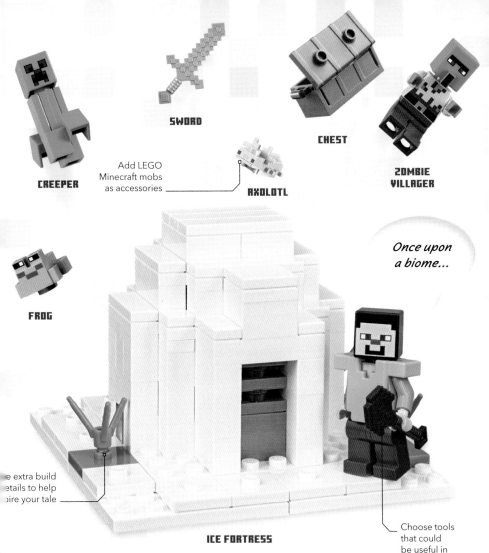

CREEPER

SWORD

CHEST

Add LEGO
Minecraft mobs
as accessories

AXOLOTL

**ZOMBIE
VILLAGER**

FROG

*Once upon
a biome...*

e extra build
etails to help
pire your tale

ICE FORTRESS

Choose tools
that could
be useful in
the story

HOW TO PLAY

1 Fill a bag with LEGO pieces, including minifigures,
accessories, and different colored bricks to
represent a selection of biomes.

2 Pull four items out of the bag: one minifigure, two
accessories, and one brick that reveals the biome
you should set your story in.

3 Build your LEGO scene in the biome. Now, take your
minifigures and accessories, and tell your own terrific
tale of adventure!

CAT

TRICKY OBSTACLES

Dash and dodge across farmland, oceans, and lava fields on this blockbusting Minecraft obstacle course. Who will be the first to make it to the ruined portal?

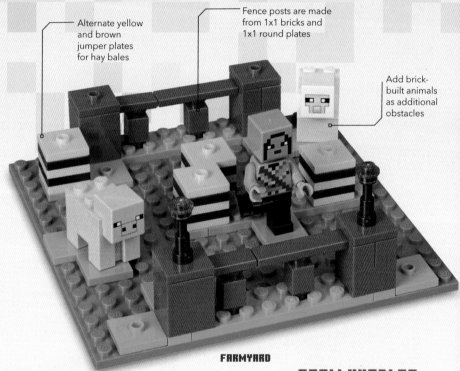

Alternate yellow and brown jumper plates for hay bales

Fence posts are made from 1x1 bricks and 1x1 round plates

Add brick-built animals as additional obstacles

FARMYARD

Go Team Steve!

FARM HURDLES

Begin the obstacle course with a farmyard frenzy. Leap over fences, zigzag through hay bales, and dodge cute creatures.

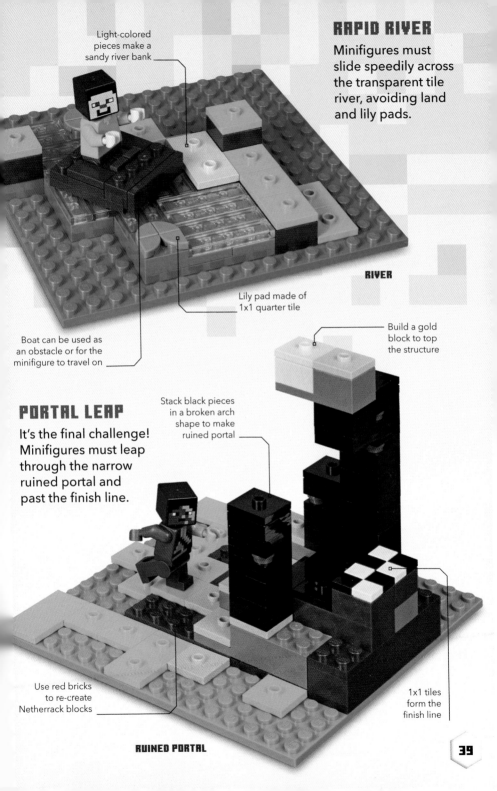

RAPID RIVER

Minifigures must slide speedily across the transparent tile river, avoiding land and lily pads.

Light-colored pieces make a sandy river bank

Lily pad made of 1x1 quarter tile

Boat can be used as an obstacle or for the minifigure to travel on

RIVER

Build a gold block to top the structure

Stack black pieces in a broken arch shape to make ruined portal

PORTAL LEAP

It's the final challenge! Minifigures must leap through the narrow ruined portal and past the finish line.

Use red bricks to re-create Netherrack blocks

1x1 tiles form the finish line

RUINED PORTAL

CATCH OF THE DAY

Start building this savanna fishing cottage and you'll soon be hooked. The little cottage is raised on stilts and juts out over a lake. What are you "baiting" for?

Burnt orange pieces look like acacia wood planks

Roof connects to 2x2 jumper plates

Hinge is made from plates with clips and plates with hooks

This fishing cottage is "reel" great!

Stacks of 1x1 bricks form stilts

Staircase built from 2x2 bricks

FARMYARD FRIENDS

In Minecraft, chickens are everywhere, providing food, feathers, and eggs. If you're a fan of these fine fowls, "peck" up your bricks and try your "cluck" at this build.

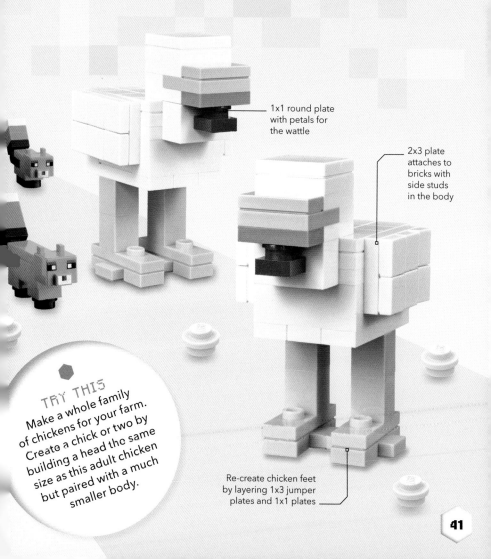

1x1 round plate with petals for the wattle

2x3 plate attaches to bricks with side studs in the body

TRY THIS
Make a whole family of chickens for your farm. Create a chick or two by building a head the same size as this adult chicken but paired with a much smaller body.

Re-create chicken feet by layering 1x3 jumper plates and 1x1 plates

DEEP SEA DISCOVERIES

Build some kelp-covered cold ocean ruins and send your minifigures glugging down to explore. Will they find gold, jewels, a treasure map, or a dreaded drowned?

Outward-facing studs re-create chiseled stone block detail

I feel like I'm getting into deep water!

Pile 1x1 round plates with peta for kelp

Use sand yellow bricks to add a hint of gold

TOWER RUIN

Create a staggered, flat roof with layered plates and tiles

MICRO RUIN

Transparent tiles look like undersea magma

Add burnt orange pieces to look like polished granite blocks

EXPANDED RUINS

Place a few of these towers, small buildings, and columns together to re-create the larger underwater ruins you can find in Minecraft's oceans.

Use light gray pieces for the ocean floor

Stack textured bricks and plates to create pillars

COLUMNS AND PILLARS

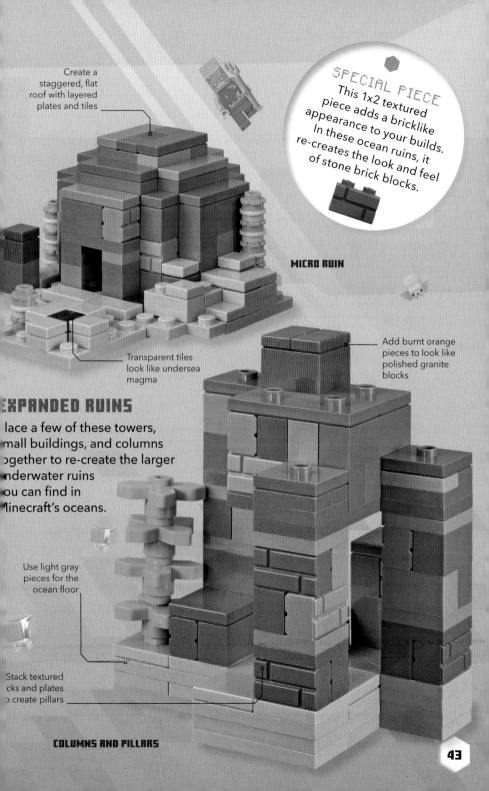

POWER UP!

In Minecraft, redstone ore provides redstone dust, which can power up blocks and items. You won't need a pickax to find LEGO redstone ore—just your LEGO bricks. Thanks to a light brick, this build really glows re

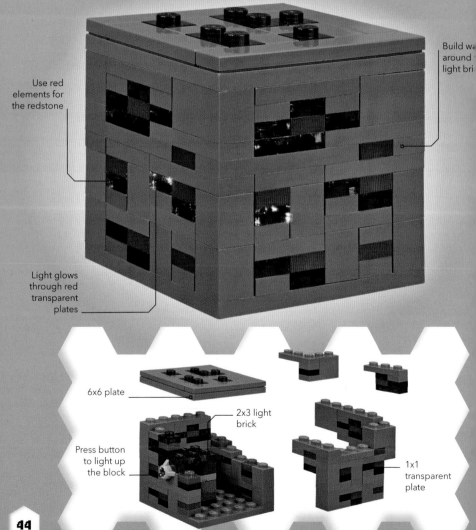

Build w
around
light bri

Use red
elements for
the redstone

Light glows
through red
transparent
plates

6x6 plate

2x3 light
brick

Press button
to light up
the block

1x1
transparent
plate

AWESOME ALLAY

Allay at your service! This helpful flying friend collects items for you. Flapping wings allow it to fly fast, and maybe dance to some Minecraft music on the way.

Large brick head is 5x5 wide and three bricks deep

TRY THIS
Allays like to dance along to music. Build a music playing device, such as a jukebox, by building a square box with a slot in the top. Add colorful tiles for different musical tunes.

Rear wings built along 1x6 plate

Stack bricks to re-create allay's uneven appearance

Front wings move up and down on ball and socket connections

45

TINY LIBRARY

This cozy library has bookshelves, lamps, oak cabinets, and a lectern. It also has a librarian who doesn't allow talking. Yes, that includes talking about LEGO Minecraft!

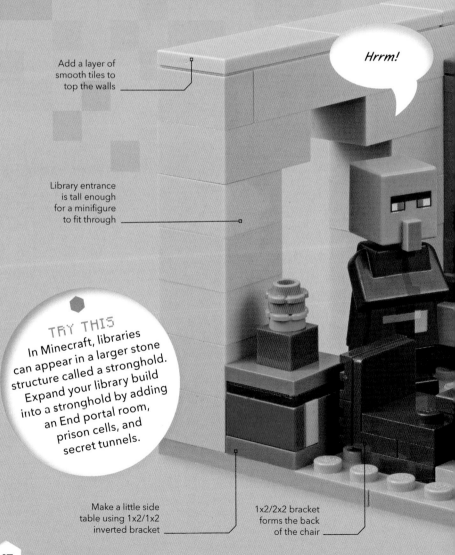

Hrrm!

Add a layer of smooth tiles to top the walls

Library entrance is tall enough for a minifigure to fit through

TRY THIS
In Minecraft, libraries can appear in a larger stone structure called a stronghold. Expand your library build into a stronghold by adding an End portal room, prison cells, and secret tunnels.

Make a little side table using 1x2/1x2 inverted bracket

1x2/2x2 bracket forms the back of the chair

1x1x1 2/3 brick
with side studs

1x2 tile

1x4 plate
with 2 studs

1x1 tile
with clip

2x4 brick

1x2 slopes
look like
the open
pages of
a book

Create drawers
with 1x1 tile handles

GROW YOUR WORLD

Cultivate a bumper batch of plants. You can re-create Minecraft trees, flowers, and crops, or use your fertile imagination to build brand-new species.

1x1 half-circle tiles form part of a lily pad

Yellow carrot-top pieces look like ripe wheat

Use 2x2 brick for dirt block plant base

LILY PAD

WHEAT

Attach tiles to 1x1 brick with four side studs to make a chorus flower

2x2 round jumper plate angled toward the sun

Stack plant pieces for a tall stem

Make End stone base from sand-colored bricks

CHORUS PLANT

SUNFLOWER

1x1 cone is central flower

TRY THIS
Why not take your floral creations to the next level and make life-size versions to decorate your home? Think about each plant's key features and how you could scale these up.

Sugar cane is up to four 1x1 round bricks tall

SUGAR CANE

TORCH FLOWER

These plants must love math— they all have square roots!

Rows of studs look like cactus spikes

Use bracket pieces for sideways building

Stack flower stems to add more flowers

CACTUS

ROSE BUSH

WEAPONSMITH VISIT

Visit the village weaponsmith for a weapons upgrade and you'll find them with their nose to the grindstone. If you're charming, they might offer you a rare weapon.

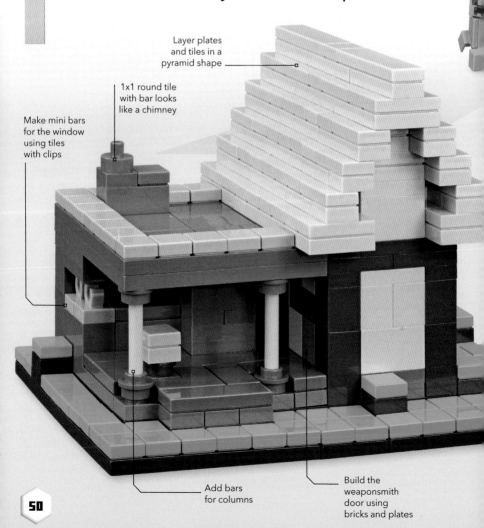

Layer plates and tiles in a pyramid shape

1x1 round tile with bar looks like a chimney

Make mini bars for the window using tiles with clips

Add bars for columns

Build the weaponsmith door using bricks and plates

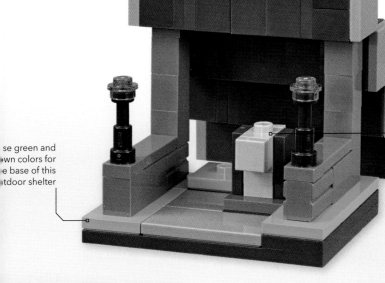

TRY THIS
Gather your LEGO pickaxes, crossbows, and swords for the weaponsmith to look at. If you don't have the accessories, build your own using bars, telescope pieces, and plates.

Stack bricks and plates to look like long logs

...se green and ...wn colors for ...e base of this ...tdoor shelter

Grindstone made from 1x1 brick with side studs, and tiles

GRINDSTONE CORNER

A weaponsmith villager uses a grindstone to craft metal into tools and weapons. Build a rustic outdoor weaponsmith with a roof made from brick-built logs and a tile dirt path.

I see a creeper, so I'm going to make a bolt for the door!

SECRET STORAGE CUBE

This isn't any old gold ore block—it's a secret hiding place for gold ingots and other treasures! Slot the pieces together to secure your secrets from nosy mobs

Gray tiles form rocky ore surface

Smooth surface hides how to take the puzzle apart

TRY THIS
Challenge yourself to make a storage cube puzzle that is harder to solve. Add an additional outer layer to your block with several sliding sides—only one will reveal the gold inside!

52

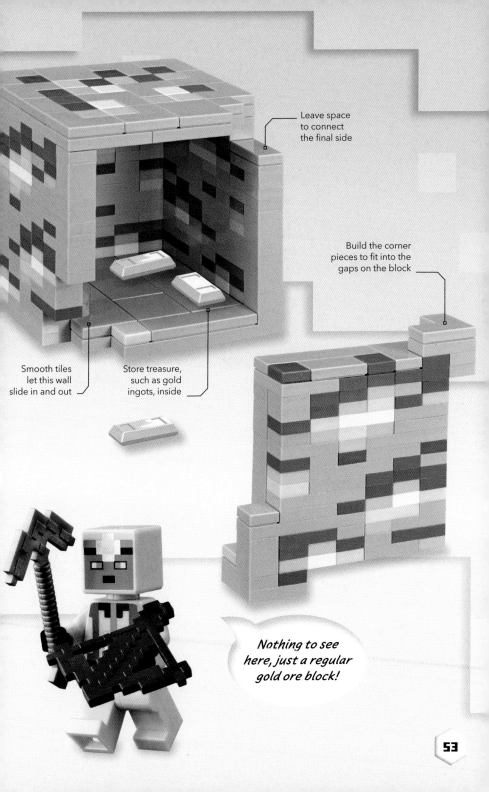

Leave space to connect the final side

Build the corner pieces to fit into the gaps on the block

Smooth tiles let this wall slide in and out

Store treasure, such as gold ingots, inside

Nothing to see here, just a regular gold ore block!

A LOT OF AXOLOTLS

This colorful bunch of axolotls will soon become your amphibian allies. Build the cute aquatic mobs with wide heads, long tails, and frilly head gills.

Add head gills in a contrasting color

BLUE AXOLOTL

Corner pieces loo like axolotl toes

1x2 plate with ball socket

1x2 plate with ball joint

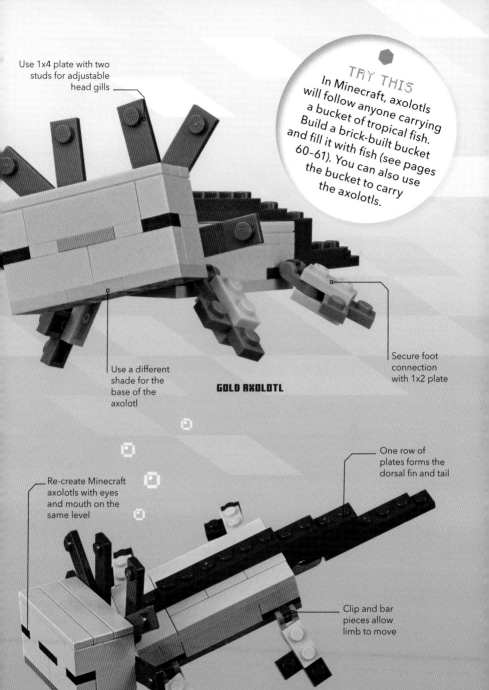

Use 1x4 plate with two studs for adjustable head gills

TRY THIS

In Minecraft, axolotls will follow anyone carrying a bucket of tropical fish. Build a brick-built bucket and fill it with fish (see pages 60–61). You can also use the bucket to carry the axolotls.

Use a different shade for the base of the axolotl

GOLD AXOLOTL

Secure foot connection with 1x2 plate

One row of plates forms the dorsal fin and tail

Re-create Minecraft axolotls with eyes and mouth on the same level

Clip and bar pieces allow limb to move

LEUCISTIC AXOLOTL

CREEPER HOUSE

Confuse hostile creepers by building a house shaped exactly like their heads. Will they make it their home, sweet home, or will they panic and creep away?

Re-create creepers' checkered pattern using different shades of green

Windows set back for 3D effect

Door handle made from 1x1 round tile

Brown flowe stem looks like dead bu

Printed TNT brick forms bedside table

Bed made from lime 2x4 plates

TOTALLY BEWITCHING

All witches will feel at home in this LEGO swamp hut. With its black cat, mushroom garden, and creepy crafting table, it's the perfect place to brew potions.

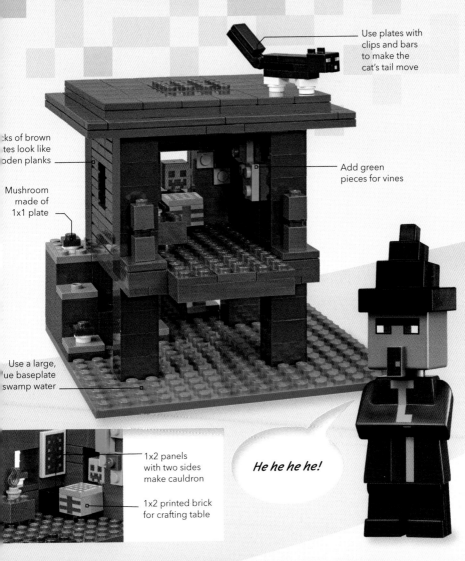

Use plates with clips and bars to make the cat's tail move

cks of brown tes look like oden planks

Add green pieces for vines

Mushroom made of 1x1 plate

Use a large, ue baseplate swamp water

1x2 panels with two sides make cauldron

1x2 printed brick for crafting table

He he he he!

SUPER SNIFFER

Grab your green and red bricks and build this seed-sniffing mob. The question is: what comes first—the egg or the fully grown sniffer?

1x2 brick with side studs

2x3 tiles

Stack pieces to re-create rectangle egg shape

Add cracks and texture by swapping bricks

SNIFFER EGG

Use tiles to re-create blocky sniffer shell

SNIFF, SNIFF!

Use 1x2x2 brick with four side studs for neck connection

Three rows of 1x3 plates for legs

POULTRY PEN POT

Build a mob as a pen pot and trust it to keep your writing implements safe. For extra fun, make its features functional, like this chicken's beak shelf.

LEGO pen

It also makes a great home for minifigures!

TRY THIS

These pots can be used for more than pens! Expand your collection with a ghast toothbrush pot, a fox plant pot, or a mooshroom pot to store minifigures.

Smooth rim made of 1x8 tiles

llow beak oubles as a shelf for stationery

Build walls to allow for maximum storage space

SOMETHING FISHY

What are you sure to see in a Minecraft sea? That's right—fish! Build a bright, bubbly school of tropical fish based on real-life fish or fin-tastical ones.

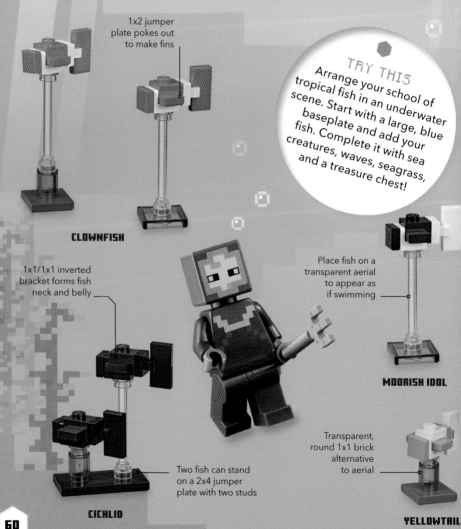

1x2 jumper plate pokes out to make fins

TRY THIS
Arrange your school of tropical fish in an underwater scene. Start with a large, blue baseplate and add your fish. Complete it with sea creatures, waves, seagrass, and a treasure chest!

CLOWNFISH

1x1/1x1 inverted bracket forms fish neck and belly

Place fish on a transparent aerial to appear as if swimming

MOORISH IDOL

Two fish can stand on a 2x4 jumper plate with two studs

Transparent, round 1x1 brick alternative to aerial

CICHLID

YELLOWTAIL PARROT

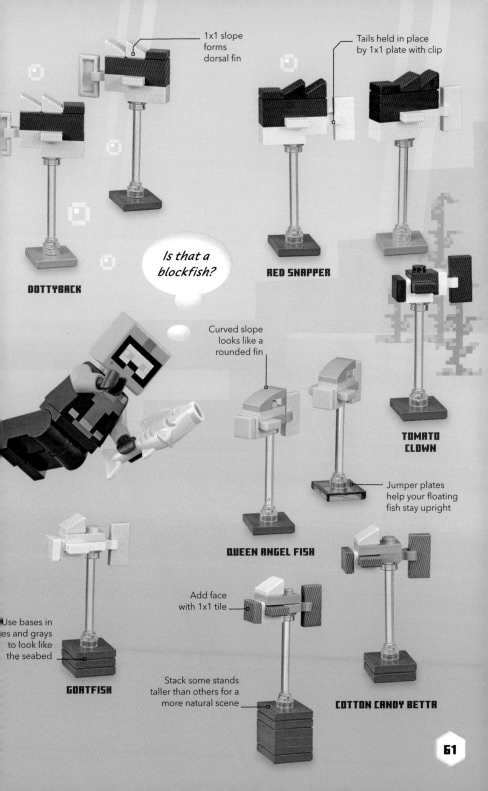

1x1 slope forms dorsal fin

Tails held in place by 1x1 plate with clip

DOTTYBACK

Is that a blockfish?

RED SNAPPER

Curved slope looks like a rounded fin

TOMATO CLOWN

Jumper plates help your floating fish stay upright

QUEEN ANGEL FISH

Use bases in es and grays to look like the seabed

GOATFISH

Add face with 1x1 tile

Stack some stands taller than others for a more natural scene

COTTON CANDY BETTA

END SHIP

All aboard the End ship! Set sail for a fabulous floating adventure above the End city in this purple micro build. It has all the details of a larger boat, but a bit less room in the cabins.

SPECIAL BRICK
This twisty unicorn horn element comes in a huge range of colors. Alongside being a horn for magical creatures, it also makes a cute microscale tree or chorus plant.

2x2 jumper plate for crow's nest

1x1 plate with clip looks like dragon figurehead

Transparent bricks for a floating effect

Layers of sand-colored plates form the End stone landscape

Horn pieces look like chorus plants

MIGHTY ENDER DRAGON

Let your imagination take flight with this large Ender Dragon. But be careful battling this fierce mob—it will defend itself with every brick, plate, and tile in its body.

Ball and socket connection allows wings to bend

Add gray tiles for scales

Articulated tail with ball and socket connections

Click hinges allow feet to move

Yikes, I want this battle to end!

1x1 tile

1x2 plate with ball joint

1x2 plate with ball socket

1x2 click hinge brick

SKELETON SHOOTERS

This target game will thrill you to the bone. The shooter is a sharp skeleton with a flick-fire missile, and the targets are three dummies. Ready, aim, fire!

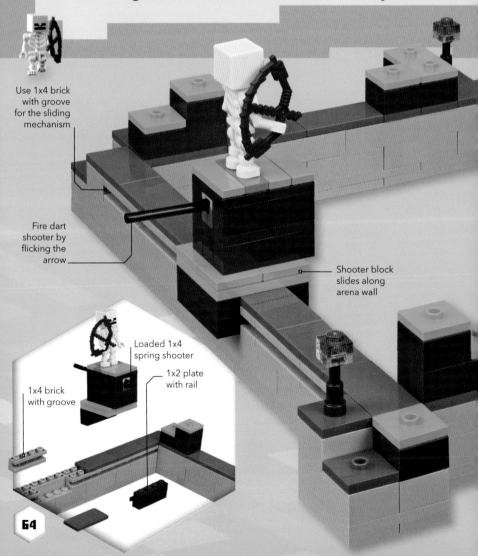

Use 1x4 brick with groove for the sliding mechanism

Fire dart shooter by flicking the arrow

Shooter block slides along arena wall

Loaded 1x4 spring shooter

1x2 plate with rail

1x4 brick with groove

HOW TO PLAY

1 Take turns to play. On your turn, slide the shooter block and aim at one of the targets. Fire!

2 If you knock down the target, your turn continues. If you miss, you'll need to start again on your next turn.

3 The first player to knock down all three targets in one turn wins.

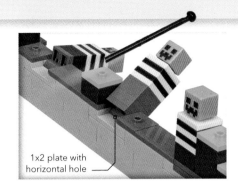

1x2 plate with horizontal hole

TOPPLING TARGETS

Leave space for your dummies in the wall and hold them in place using 1x2 plates with holes attached to nearby bricks using a pin. When hit, the targets topple backward.

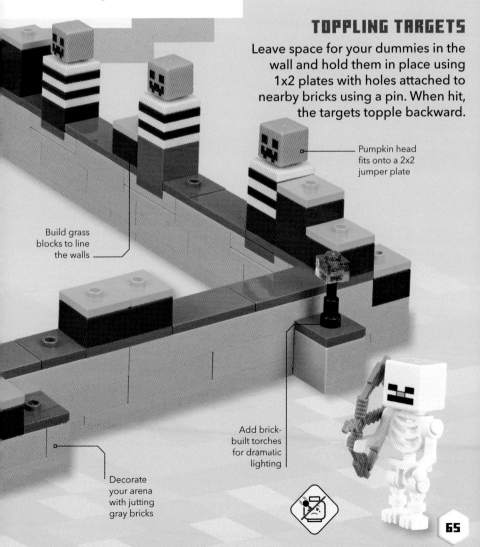

Pumpkin head fits onto a 2x2 jumper plate

Build grass blocks to line the walls

Add brick-built torches for dramatic lighting

Decorate your arena with jutting gray bricks

PYRAMID MYSTERY

Do you like digging into the mysteries of history? Then build this desert pyramid filled with secret rooms, loot, and TNT traps to foil intruders. It's simply sand-tastic!

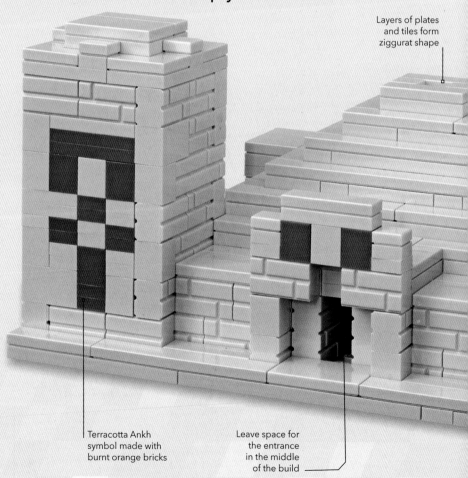

Layers of plates and tiles form ziggurat shape

Terracotta Ankh symbol made with burnt orange bricks

Leave space for the entrance in the middle of the build

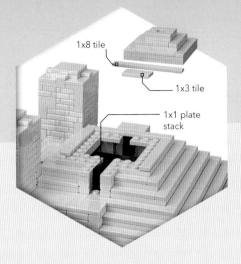

1x8 tile

1x3 tile

1x1 plate stack

TRY THIS

This pyramid can hide more than just loot and traps! Build a mysterious treasure and conceal it inside your pyramid model. Then challenge your friends and family to a treasure hunt to find it.

1x2 textured brick forms crumbling pyramid walls

TRAP OR TREASURE?

This loot-filled room has a secret. Beneath the floor, there are TNT bricks ready to explode if a minifigure steps on the pressure plate. Recreate this hidden trap by building half a room so you can see the layers underground.

Loot chest made of 2x2 brick and jumper plate

Gray tile looks like pressure plate

TNT TNT TNT

INTERIOR SCENE

Base is made by g multiple plates of different sizes

DASH FOR THE DRAGON

Challenge your friends to a race to defeat the Ender Dragon. Dodge creepers, spiders, and more, to save the Overworld and ensure it's all over for the dragon.

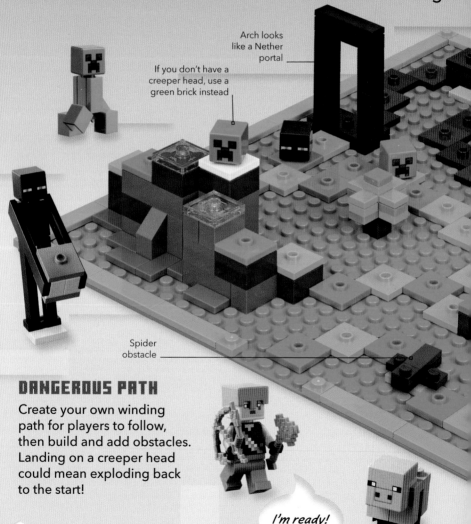

Arch looks like a Nether portal

If you don't have a creeper head, use a green brick instead

Spider obstacle

DANGEROUS PATH

Create your own winding path for players to follow, then build and add obstacles. Landing on a creeper head could mean exploding back to the start!

I'm ready!